Nunnington Hall
Yorkshire, England.

D1013066

Pot
Pourri
and other
Scented Delights

For Emma Mary

Pot
Pourri
and other
Scented Delights

Reginald Peplow

Illustrated by Carol Smith

THE NATIONAL TRUST

UNWIN HYMAN

London   Sydney

First published in Great Britain by Unwin
Hyman,
an imprint of Unwin Hyman Limited, 1987.

Published in association with The National Trust
for Places of Historic Interest or Natural Beauty.

UNWIN HYMAN LIMITED
Denmark House, 37–39 Queen Elizabeth Street
London SE1 2QB
and
40 Museum Street
London WC1A 1LU

Allen & Unwin Australia Pty Ltd
8 Napier Street, North Sydney, NSW 2060,
Australia

Allen & Unwin New Zealand Pty Ltd
with the Port Nelson Press
60 Cambridge Terrace, Wellington, New Zealand

British Library Cataloguing in Publication Data
Peplow, Reginald
  Pot pourri: and other scented delights.
  1. Perfumes   2. Flowers—Drying
  I. Title   II. National Trust
  745.92   TP983

  ISBN 0–04–440045–4

Designed by **Elizabeth Palmer**
Typeset by **Latimer Trend & Company Ltd,
Plymouth**
Printed in Great Britain by
William Clowes Ltd, Beccles and London

Contents

Introduction

In mediaeval and Elizabethan times, people knew the value of herbs. Herbs were an essential part of everyday life, removing warts, quietening a rumbling stomach, guarding against pestilence and plague and putting witches to flight. But there was a gentler more enjoyable side to herbs. They became associated with a recognized language and with careful arrangement could spell out messages of friendship and love. Herbs were boiled, burnt and baked as flavourings for wine and cider and their oils extracted

to make heady fragrances.

The happy and subtle employment of herbs will be disclosed anew. This book will encourage you to bring the fragrance of the garden into your house. If no herbs grow in your garden, then your misfortune or error can be rectified with the help of the seeds and plants revealed to you. If you have no garden of your own and rely on friends for petals, leaves and seeds, there is still much to learn.

In adopting the ideas and following the recipes in this book you will be following in the footsteps of your ancestors for whom pot pourri, sleep pillows and even love charms were among the accepted pleasures of life.

In her stillroom, the mistress of the house and other members of the family made the soaps, skin lotions, candles, air fresheners and numerous other items which most of us now buy. She required neither cookery book nor herbal since valuable knowledge had been handed down to her from past generations. Fortunately for us, she often made notes to remind herself and it is these stillroom records which have yielded many of the recipes in use today.

Making pot pourri and

other scented delights is not an
act of pure nostalgia as you
will be gathering and using
herbs to meet the needs of
today, but as you do so, do
not forget their history.

Pot Pourri

For centuries petals of scented roses and other sweet smelling flowers have been gathered and used to make what is still called pot pourri. This is traditionally a mixture of plant materials including petals, fragrant leaves, seeds and powdered roots to which are added essential oils and a selection of spices.

The finished product, (pronounced poe pooree) always gives great pleasure, but the creative processes involved are equally enjoyable. Making the mixture is surprisingly easy and children in particular are fascinated by the rituals of gathering, blending and shaking.

Before setting about the task, ask yourself how you will use the pot pourri. Perhaps you want a mixture which will scent a room in the winter and bring back memories of the lazy, hazy days of summer. You may require a fragrance to keep linen and clothing 'country fresh' or to help you drop gently off to sleep. Alternatively you may need to banish dog and cat smells or to chase off moths, ants and other pests.

As you become more experienced in the art of making pot pourri you will find you are able to create fragrant and colourful mixes for these and many other purposes.

Rose petals are favourite
Rose petals are the favourite ingredient of most pot pourris and the more colourful and perfumed they are, the more effective and delightful the result will be. If you have only a small selection or perhaps no rose bushes at all, ask neighbours to let you collect from their bushes just before the petals drop.

As long as a flower or leaf has a pleasant aroma or an attractive colour when dried, it can be used for making pot pourri. Delphinium and chamomile flowers are particularly suitable, as are the heads, leaves and broken stems of lavender, the leaves of lemon verbena, pineapple sage and marjoram, and the many varieties of fragrant thyme.

The great joy of making pot pourri is that there are no firm rules so never be afraid to experiment. You will find that the petals of sunflowers and marigolds dry well and add colour. Mint is another candidate but must be used with caution, as it has a particularly powerful aroma when dried and does not please everyone.

Harvesting

Gather plant material at a time when there is little or no moisture in the air. Use one or more baskets and avoid mixing various petals, leaves and stems at this stage as each may require different drying methods. It is considered best to pick rose heads during one sally into the garden, coloured flowers at another, and so on. The danger is that you will gather more than you can dry with ease and be left with a nasty, soggy mess instead of crisp, sweet-smelling ingredients for your pot pourri.

Roses are of no use for your purpose when they are still in bud or have faded. Gather them when they retain their scent and colour but are well open and have given their best. Use one hand to hold the stem firmly just under the base of the head and with the other give the head a quick twist. All the petals will come away in your hand and fall apart as you put them gently into the basket.

Gather other plant material as it suits you. If you have plenty of choice, cut the flowers or leaves at the bottom of the stalks so that you may hang them in the sun to dry. If you are in short supply, remove heads and leaves from the plants and place them in a basket.

Find an uncluttered surface and sort through your collection, discarding any petals or leaves that are diseased, faded, distorted or otherwise unattractive to behold. Remove leaves from stalks and petals from flower heads.

Drying

The traditional way to dry delicate rose petals, flowers and leaves for pot pourri is to spread them loosely on old newspaper in an airy place. A spare bedroom or loft floor with the window slightly open is ideal for this purpose. However, do be careful to warn visitors not to open the door suddenly, as this may create a draught which will scatter your precious gatherings everywhere.

If possible, tie your plants loosely by their stems and hang them up to dry in a porch or near a window, or lay them out on paper in an airing cupboard or shed. Paper or a tray is nearly always necessary, otherwise you may lose material and at

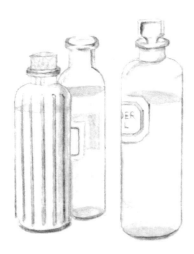

the same time run the risk of spreading plant dust everywhere.

The drying process will take up to a week. After a day or so, the leaves and petals will have shrivelled and reduced in size, which is a good sign. Stir them gently to ensure that both sides dry evenly and separate any that have become joined together.

Once your petals and leaves are what is described as 'papery' and obviously free of moisture, you must ensure that they remain dry until you are ready to use them. They are best stored in airtight containers or in brown paper bags in a damp-free drawer or the airing cupboard. Strip heads and leaves from stems and stalks which have been hung to dry and store these in a similar way.

Other ingredients

If you have not already done so, begin gathering together the other ingredients for your pot pourri and keep your eyes open for suitable bowls and containers.

For a simple pot pourri you will need some orris root powder as a fixative and a small phial of an essential oil. Both are available from good herbalists, chemists and other suppliers.

If you want your pot pourri to be completely home made, as in the days when the monks made aromatic mixes to help the sick who visited their gates, you can make your own oils. Advice on how to do this can be found on pages 72 and 73.

The fixative most commonly employed nowadays is called orris root. If you want to save money, but not time, you can make your own by cultivating the pale blue Iris *florentina*. Like other members of the iris family they are grown from roots, called rhizomes, which should be planted with a covering of about 3cm, an inch of soil and dug up after flowering in the third year. Replant the slender outer pieces and save the thick parts to be scrubbed clean, peeled, dried in a warm place and stored safe from mice and insects for two years. It takes this time for the sweet, violet-like scent to develop. The rhizomes become rock-like and may need a few blows from a hammer before they can be crushed into a powder.

The roots of angelica, sweet cicely and geranium can also be used as fixatives. Other beautifully aromatic fixatives are gum benzoin, which is a tree resin, and the tonka (also called tonquin) bean, once used to give vanilla-like fragrance to snuffs and tobacco. The bean is regarded by some herbalists as having the most concentrated floral odour which can be overpoweringly sweet.

Essential oil is the concentrated essence extracted from the flowering parts, seeds, bark, leaves and roots of numerous plants. It is the natural aroma which can be released simply by crushing a plant between two fingers and rupturing the cells.

There are hundreds of oils from which to choose, all of them extremely aromatic, and it would be advisable to start with half a dozen or less. Those recommended are lavender (fresh and piercing), rosemary (refreshing), bergamot (a hint of orange), rose geranium (the scent of roses), lemon verbena (more than a hint of lemon) and sandalwood (sweet and

persistent).

As you begin to devise and mix your own pot pourris, you will quickly appreciate the power of essential oil. Great restraint must be exercised so that you avoid ruining the delicate balance of your mix. What you will also discover is that by blending your oils, or by buying them blended, you have control over the degree of floral, fresh, spicy and woody fragrances that will surround and hopefully excite you.

Begin to look at recipes handed down over the centuries. Try looking for old books in libraries. Do not despair when one calls for, say, grains of musk, you can buy essence of musk as a useful substitute. Apart from fixatives and oils, some recipes call for small quantities of ground cloves, cinnamon and all spice and citrus peel. There should be no problem in finding these.

Sample oils on a sliver of wood or scrap of blotting paper rather than on your fingers or wrist. Always wear rubber gloves when handling strong oils to avoid skin reactions. You can accidentally smell like a perfumery counter for days unless you take care, and clothing could well become impregnated.

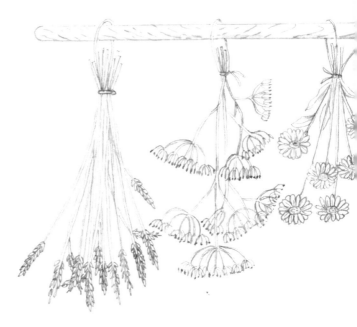

Making pot Pourri

Take a large china bowl and pour into this several handfuls of the dried rose petals with smaller quantities of whatever dried flower petals and leaves you have available. Stir them up and continue to add plant material to provide a texture and colour which is satisfying.

Sprinkle a single drop of essential oil over the surface and stir gently with a piece of stick. Add another drop and stir, and then four more drops, stirring between each drop. Next, add about a teaspoon of orris root powder, which is the fixative, to every five handfuls

of the plant material, and stir once again. The combination of the plant aroma, the oil and the fixative is almost certain to make you pleasantly light-headed, but never add so much oil that your creation scents the air too heavily.

Stirring is best done with a stick or old wooden spoon which may then be kept with the pot pourri or discarded. Household implements will retain the aroma of the oil for a long time so should not be used.

You must now find some means of keeping it airtight. The main point is that the

will add to your enjoyment of it in later years.

This is known as the dry method of making pot pourri. There is also the wet method, from which the term pot pourri (rotted pot) comes. This method is inclined to be complicated, time-consuming and messy, and is now less popular. However, there is an argument that the wet method produces a more subtle fragrance. The basic procedure is to take rose petals (dried in the manner already described), and pack them into a large crock with salt and leave for several weeks before adding fixatives.

container has a tight fitting lid and that it will not absorb moisture. Biscuit tins are frowned upon, but lined with newspaper serve marvellously, and plastic containers are also useful.

Pour the raw pot pourri into the container of your choice and store in a warm place where you can reach it easily. Shake it for a few moments every day for six weeks, and from then on just occasionally until you are ready to use the pot pourri. If you can find time to label the container with the date of mixing and nature of mix, this

How to use your pot pourri

One good way to use your simple pot pourri is to keep it in a pretty lidded china bowl. Once the lid is removed, it will give a room that natural aroma which is evocative of the days when you first picked your roses and laid the petals out to dry.

Pot pourri may also be kept in a glass bowl which reveals more readily the subtle mixture of colours. This effect can be accentuated by the addition of a complete rose bud or pretty flower head.

If well made, pot pourri will retain its heady aroma for

many years. But if it does seem to be fading, revive it by adding a few drops of essential oil and half a tablespoon of orris root powder. Give it a good shaking every day for seven days and then remove from the light for a couple of weeks.

Where a pot pourri is to be used as a moth or general insect repellent, you will need to include other dried herbs such as wormwood, tansy and meadowsweet.

Fragrant Herbs and Flowers

Here is a selection of flowers and herbs with fragrant petals, seeds and leaves which are ideal for pot pourri:

    Angelica (leaves)

    Anise (seeds)

    Basil (leaves)

Bay (leaves)

Coriander (seeds)

Lavender (leaves and seeds)

Lemon balm (leaves)

Lemon geranium (leaves)

Lemon thyme (leaves)

Lemon verbena (leaves)

Marjoram (leaves)

Orange mint (leaves)

Peppermint (leaves)

Pineapple sage (leaves)

Pinks (petals)

Rose (petals)

Rose geranium (leaves)

Rosemary (leaves)

Strawberry (leaves)

Tansy (flowers and leaves)

Tarragon (leaves)

Woodruff (leaves)

For colourful petals, try the following:

Bachelor's button

Bergamot

Blue mallow

Borage

Calendula

Chamomile

Daffodil

Delphinium

Forsythia

Honeysuckle

Jasmine

Larkspur

Lavender

Marigold

Pansy

Pinks

Viola

Violet

Wallflowers

Zinnia

Zonal geranium

When sleep eludes you and counting sheep has lost its appeal, try going to bed with some sweet scented herbs beneath your head. You will almost certainly drift into a peaceful slumber. When you awake in the morning you will be surrounded by the gently evocative scents from the gardens you know and love and the day takes on a brighter prospect.

You have to chose the right aromatic herbs, of course, and this is where you can prove your newly acquired skills. Follow the basic methods described in the previous chapter, but be sure to add a cupful of dried lavender to the mixture. However, if you are a hardened insomniac and know the names and distinguishing marks of every ewe and ram in the flock, a special mix is required.

You will need to make the pot pourri from equal measures (a cup perhaps) of rosemary and marjoram, and half-measures of lemon thyme and spearmint. Add the fixative and essential oil, lavender would be best, together with a well crushed stick of cinnamon and the dried and powdered peel of an orange.

When you have shaken the

pot pourri for a few weeks, it will be cured. Sew it into a loosely woven cloth bag measuring 22 × 15cm, 9 × 6in and place this between the slip and the pillow so that the warmth of a head resting on it will release the fragrance.

As with all other types of pot pourri, there is plenty of room for experiment. You may find that the leaves of the tiny herb sweet woodruff

combined with those of the exceptionally aromatic lemon verbena are sufficient on their own without oil and fixative. Some people swear by hops, others cannot abide them.

Pillows as presents

If you want to give sleep pillows as presents, make them as described and chose a pretty, but light fabric as an outer slip cover which can be removed for washing.

The secret of success with herb pillows is to produce a pot pourri which will please the hopeful sleeper. Once the perfume is liked and accepted, it offers a hint of welcome and warmth which, in itself, can help to promote sleep. Bed is then no longer a place to toss and turn, it becomes a haven, somewhere to close the eyes and think of lovely things and maybe happier times.

Pillow of love
Traditionally, not all herb pillows were for insomniacs. Looking through an old herbal recently I found a recipe for a

'pillow of love'. You will need
four parts of dried violet
flowers, three parts of dried
rose petals (highly scented),
one part tonquin beans (for
their extreme sweetness) and
one part orris root powder.
Make the pot pourri as
described earlier and hope for
the best.

American settlers found
herb pillows very useful for
relieving headaches and
banishing melancholy. A
Midwestern pioneer recipe
called for a mix of two parts

each of lavender, marjoram, rose petals and betony, and 14g, $\frac{1}{2}$oz of cloves. A simpler mix was two parts rose petals, one part mint and 7g, $\frac{1}{4}$oz of crushed clove.

Cushions

It is not just in the bedroom that a touch of summer fragrance is welcome—herb cushions are coming into their own again. Not only comforting, they encourage repose for those who find life a little too stressful.

Invalids and the elderly derive great relief from resting with a perfumed cushion

behind or beneath them. Patients in hospital wards, surrounded as they are by unaccustomed sights and clinical smells, can find solace in the presence of a gently aromatic cushion which gives pleasure during a long day and maybe even longer night.

Lavender is of particular value here; its aroma is familiar and has the ability to soothe frayed nerves. It can be used on its own in a small bag of porous material to be tucked within the cushion, or added generously to a matured, basic pot pourri.

If lavender is unacceptable,

and shapes—circles, oblongs and hearts. Those for practical use about the house were normally about 15cm, 6in square.

Their principal use was to perfume linen either on the bed or in store. They were also tucked into corners of cupboards and drawers and hung from hooks and hangers among the out-of-season garments in clothes closets. It was the custom in some houses to tie sweet bags to the back of chairs so that they released their fragrance when leant against.

There is no firm recipe, but obviously the aroma is of more importance than the colour. A simple pot pourri which gives out an attractively sharp, lemon scent is made from four parts each of lemon verbena leaves, lavender flowers and scented geranium leaves with one part peppermint, a teaspoon of orris root powder and a drop or two of essential oil (lemon verbena).

It is usual to crush the pot pourri into powder before inserting it into the sachets. Do this with an old rolling pin, piece of wood, or a pestle and mortar. Crushing is not essential, but you may well feel that the scent is more noticeable if you do.

an alternative is to make a pot pourri of equal parts of peppermint, sage and lemon balm with smaller quantities of such herbs as lemon thyme, woodruff, rosemary and red bergamot. Other ingredients could include a touch of angelica, lemon verbena, lemon thyme and marjoram.

Perfumed sachets and sweet bags

The mistress of the house used to make what she called sweet bags. These were easy to make and very effective in lending a fresh scent when stored with linen. They were of all sizes

Personal Care

Aromatic herbal baths

The Romans scented their bath water by throwing in large quantities of aromatic herbs, and the pleasure derived from this is as applicable now as it was then. The only difference is that you can save time, trouble and mess by enclosing the herbs in cheesecloth bags and hanging one from the hot tap so that the water runs through it.

Such a procedure has been followed for centuries, and some of the greatest beauties have attributed the continuance of their charms over the years to leisurely bathing in scented herbal water. One French beauty who kept her attractions well over pension age was said to dip regularly in a 'magic water' containing a muslin bag of lavender leaves, rosemary and mint with comfrey roots.

Apart from keeping clean and beautiful, there are of course many reasons for taking a bath. There are also many sweet scented herbs you may use to help you achieve the purpose you have in mind.

If you arrive home tired and literally aching for a good hot bath, try a mixture of sage and strawberry leaves with a little lemon verbena to improve the scent. For a bath to lift the spirits, try a mix of four parts lavender flowers and one part lovage leaves.

All aromatic herbs are good in the bath and you will soon be able to invent your own mixtures. Leaves of spearmint and thyme in equal measures make an excellent combination. Experiment with the roots of herbs, particularly angelica and lovage, and add lemon peel, cloves and cinnamon to see how it affects your mood.

The Romans, who were not shy when it came to making the most of brotherly and sisterly love, used pennyroyal to scent their bath water before a night on the tiles. In most cases, they steeped the herb with others in small quantities of boiling water and stored the fragrant liquid in jars. An infusion of this sort may well be more attractive than bags.

Taking the waters

If you ever get the idea that toilet waters and body oils are slightly decadent, remember that some of the earliest used were invented by Carmelite nuns in France. They made

fragrant and refreshing waters from a number of natural ingredients including lemon balm, angelica, lemon peel, coriander and oriental spices.

The nuns may well have taken the idea from the Queen of Hungary who, apparently, learnt from a hermit a wonderfully easy way to restore the use of paralysed limbs and at the same time bring back beauty. It appeared to work, for according to legend, she was nearly eighty when she eventually caught the eye of the King of Poland in the thirteenth century.

The Queen's special mixture, Hungary water, requires a distillation process but simple and refreshing cologne along the same lines can be made with a few handfuls of herbs from your garden.

A simple, but extremely refreshing toilet water can be made by soaking rose petals in a cup of vodka for a week. At the end of this process, crush roughly equal quantities of fresh basil and peppermint leaves, with a little grated orange peel, and steep this in boiling water. When this is cool, strain the rose leaves and the herbs, mix both liquids and store in an airtight bottle.

Dusting powder

The usefulness of herbs does not stop when you finally emerge, glowing, from your bath; the rejuvenating process continues with sweetly scented dusting powder. Herbs can not only give you a glow when you are in the bath, they can spice up your life afterwards in the form of sweet dusting powders.

You can make a most effective powder by pounding to a powder and blending together dried rose petals, dried lavender buds and a little orris root powder and then adding the equivalent amount of cornflower.

Fragrant skin lotion

Here is a way of making a deliciously soft lotion for your skin. Infuse a few handfuls of elderflower or marigold flowers in boiling water and leave overnight. Carefully strain, and than dissolve a teaspoon of borax in this infusion. Warm two teaspoons of ground nut oil and add

slowly, beating until the mixture emulsifies. Finally, add two drops of essential oil of lavender.

Breath sweeteners

To make your breath clean and attractive, chew a small piece of angelica root. But if you have access to the wine cupboard, here is a more effective remedy passed down over the years.

Take half a pint of sherry wine and into this put 28g, 1oz each of powdered cloves, grated nutmeg, and 14g, $\frac{1}{2}$oz each of ground cinnamon and bruised caraway seeds. Place all this in a flask and allow to stand for three days, shaking the mixture well twice a day. Finally, strain the liquid through a cheesecloth and add ten drops of spirits of lavender. Pour a few drops of the liquid onto a lump of sugar for fragrant breath or add a drop or two to water to make a first class gargle.

Another sweet mouthwash is made from an infusion of lemon verbena, lavender, marigold, marjoram, peppermint, rosemary, sage or thyme.

If you would like to try cleaning your teeth as our ancestors did, and perhaps benefit from the aromatic experience, rub them with fresh sage leaves.

For the eyes

Aromatic eye washes may be unusual but they have a soothing effect. A fragrant infusion of the leaves of herbs such as chamomile, coltsfoot, eyebright, fennel, lemon verbena, marigold, marshmallow, parsley, and raspberry is much to be recommended. Use a sponge to wipe the liquid gently over the eyelids. Another soothing method of application is to soak pieces of clean lint, cotton or cotton wool in the infusion and lay them over the eyes for a while. Or you may prefer to make tiny sachets, filled with the herbs and

soaked in warm water to lay
on the eyes.

Herbs for the feet

If 'Oh, my poor feet' is a
phrase frequently on your lips,
indulge in an aromatic foot
bath. A gentle soak in
fragrant herbs will pamper the
feet and rest the mind.
Lavender steeped in boiling
water is also most effective and
can be combined with
marigold leaves. Alternatively,
try putting a handful or two
of nettle leaves, rosemary,
lavender and mint into boiling
water, adding a pinch of
crushed or powdered mustard
seed.

A good recipe from 1775
requires four handfuls each of
pennyroyal, sage and
rosemary, three handfuls of
angelica and 113g, 4oz of
juniper berries. Boil the
ingredients in a sufficient
quantity of water and strain
off the liquid for use.

Aromatic hair care

Sweet smelling herbs are used
to add fragrance and lustre to
hair. Start by making a simple
sweet-smelling rinse, which
encourages an attractive glossy
appearance.

Use rosemary on dark hair
and chamomile on light hair.
Take a handful of rosemary

leaves or chamomile flowers
and steep them in boiling
water for half an hour. Strain
through muslin into an
earthenware jug and cover
once cool. Use as the final
rinse after washing, by
pouring it several times over
your head into a basin.

To darken grey hair, collect
a small handful of rosemary
leaves and an equal quantity
of sage leaves and mix these
with a teaspoonful of tea
leaves (or a couple of tea
bags) in an earthenware jug.
Pour boiling water over them,
and use this as a rinse when
cool.

Nettles can be used to make
a rinse which tackles dandruff
while giving hair a real gloss.
Use gloves to gather them
fresh and then steep them
overnight in boiling water.
When cool, add a quarter cup
each of cider, vinegar and eau
de Cologne. Massage this into
the scalp two or three times a
week.

If you grow the herb
soapwort, a great cleanser,
now used for cleaning old
tapestries and oil paintings,
you can make your own
shampoo. Put some small
pieces of the root into a pan
and immerse in boiling water.
Let it steep for thirty minutes,
then strain. When it is cool,

take a cupful of the liquid and mix in the beaten yolk of an egg. Use only warm water to shampoo your hair; if it is too hot, the egg will scramble.

In Shakespeare's day, young men rubbed their chins with the aromatic southernwood in the hope of making their beards grow faster. Older men used the herb on their heads to help cure them of their baldness.

There is a fortune awaiting anyone able to promise luxuriant growth of hair for the balding. It is said that the pungent catmint, made into an infusion and used in the rinsing water, will increase hair growth but, alas, will not bring back hair that has fallen out. An eighteenth century recipe calls for the infusion of a handful of rosemary in four teacupfuls of white wine for a day and a night and the addition of almond oil. A more modern suggestion is that those with thinning hair should slice an onion, cover it with unsweetened gin and after a day begin massaging a little of the mixture into the roots. The green leaves of the Jerusalem artichoke are said to be good for the bald patch when stewed in a little water for three hours, and daffodil leaves and flowers are said to have the same effect, but there are many sceptics.

Sweet Delights

Washballs and soaps

Like throwing pottery, soap making offers an excellent excuse for enjoying a singularly messy hour or two with the advantage of having something for family or friends at the end of the day.

Housewives of the seventeenth century, unable to afford the highly scented offerings of the perfumers of the time, made their own from sweet smelling herbs gathered from their gardens or from the meadows and hedgerows. They were rewarded for their labours in the long run as perfumers were adding arsenic, white lead and mercury 'to soften the skin and whiten the complexion'!

Start by making herbal wash balls. These were very popular before bars of soap, as we know them, came on to the market and do not require elaborate equipment or expensive ingredients.

The basic ingredients are two bars of glycerine or unscented soap, a cup of floral water and a few drops of an essential oil of your choice. To make the floral water, infuse fragrant rose petals or one or more sweetly scented herbs such as mint, lemon balm, lemon verbena and chamomile in boiling water, leave to cool and then strain.

Put thin strips of the soap into a mixing bowl and pour over about half a cupful of warmed floral water. Leave this for about a quarter of an hour and then stir. Finally, pour the substance into your blender or give it a vigorous mix by hand. While doing so, add a few drops of essential oil one drop at a time.

Allow the mixture to cool then pour it into a container, such as a pudding bowl and allow it to set. When the soap is firm, but not completely dried out (it takes about two days), scoop it out, as you might ice cream, and mould it into a golf ball form.

Leave the balls in the sun or in a warm room and when they are almost dry, dip your hands into the cool floral water and rub each ball in turn between your palms to give the surface a smooth and polished finish.

Home-made wash balls might not save money but the skin, particular uncovered areas like face and hands, will benefit considerably from the change to a pure, naturally scented product you have made yourself.

Incense and cones

'One should be sure night and morning to perfume the house with angelica seeds, burnt in a fire-pan or chafing dish of coales' was the sound counsel offered to careful householders in 1661. It still applies today, but follow the advice by introducing aromatic herbs from the garden rather than by breaking every safety code and putting house, family and worldly goods at risk.

An interesting way to perfume the house in winter is

to stick dried lavender stems (with their flower heads but no leaves) into a container of sand, small pebbles or flower arranger's oasis. Place this in the hallway or a selected room and light the tips. The lavender will burn very slowly giving out a wonderous aromatic smoke.

What a writer in 1662 called 'an odoriferous perfume for chambers' is highly effective. Mix a quarter pint of floral rose water (see page 73) with a tablespoon of powdered cloves and store this in a jam jar, out of the light, for a few days to mature. When required, sprinkle a few drops every hour or so onto a hot, dry, iron pan so the scent gently fills the room.

A 'boiling perfume' much loved by Edward VI, reigned 1547–53, was made in the following way:

> *[Take] 12 spoonfuls of bright red rose-water, the weight of 6 pence in fine powder sugar, and boil it on hot embers and coals softly, and the room will smell as though it were full of roses; but you must burn sweet cyprus wood before to take away the gross air.*

If you are lucky enough to discover an incense burner in your local antique shop or market, use it to burn small pieces of dried rosemary, sage and southernwood. These herbs have been much valued through the ages for their antiseptic qualities and modern science supports that age-old view.

The effect can be achieved more simply outside in the summer, when you have a barbecue. Wait for the charcoal to glow and drop on a piece of dried herb of the woody variety, like lavender and rosemary.

Pine cones with a little added perfume can make a room look and smell rich and festive. Find some dry, well-opened cones and using a small paint brush, coat them very thinly with cooking oil until they glisten. With the same brush, paint a few drops of an essential oil of your choice into the crevices of each cone. Pile the cones into a colourful basket or decorate them with ribbons and hang them over the fireplace. As the room warms from the fire, central heating or sun, the cones will emit a gentle aroma.

The candle's glow
When making candles you may use aromatic dried herbs which you have harvested and

stored or freshly picked heads, leaves and stems. Lemon scented herbs release a particularly pleasing aroma in a burning candle, but always experiment with other herbs.

Make a sachet of loosely woven material with a short tape or string attached to one end, then sew your chosen herbs into it. At the same time, search out burnt-down candle ends of any colour and a clean plastic yoghurt pot or similar container to use as a mould. Coat the inside of the pot with cooking oil, to prevent the wax from sticking, and punch a small hole in the bottom with a pencil.

Attach a piece of string to the pencil and balance it over the open mouth of the pot so it hangs centrally. Thread the other end of the string through the hole in the bottom of the pot and cut it leaving about 3cm, 1in. Pull the string taut and then block the hole with sticky tape or plasticine.

Remove all traces of wick from the old candles and, with great care, heat them up in the top section of a double saucepan. To introduce the fragrance, drop the sachet of herbs into the pan with the tape or string hanging over the edge. When the wax

reaches a temperature of about 82° centigrade, 180° fahrenheit, remove the sachet and pour the liquid into the pot taking care not to disturb the string.

When the wax has hardened, remove the mould and the candle is ready for burning.

Even white household candles can be made to smell and look more interesting by decorating them with the flowers, leaves and seeds of herbs. The plant material used for this should be dried and pressed, so some advance planning is needed.

Pin the leaves and flowers lightly to each candle and then heat the ends of old white candles or paraffin wax in a jar over boiling water in a saucepan. Using a small brush, paint the hot liquid over the candle and the pinned herbs. Work with long, firm strokes to achieve a transparent coating in minimum time. Remove the pins and you will find the herbs are sealed into the candle.

When you light the candle, the flowers will take on a fascinating, translucent appearance and the aroma will be just discernible, yet delightful.

Pomanders

In the days when foul smells and pestilence attacked the nostrils and weakened the limbs, eminent people like Mary Queen of Scots or Cardinal Wolsey, rarely ventured forth without a pomander tied to their belts.

The pomanders used by the

rich and aristocratic were often made of rare, scented resins and a host of recipes for making pomanders have been handed down over the centuries. The resins were frequently enclosed in a hollow ball made of openwork metal (Mary's was silver) through which the scent could escape and supposedly ward off surrounding evils.

When citrus fruits were introduced to this country, physicians and others visiting the sick carried pomanders made from the scooped out skin of the fruit filled with aromatic herbs and spices. Others used an orange with its skin pressed full of cloves, and this simple device soon became popular as an attractive gift for friends. Nowadays, people do not string their precious pomanders from their belts but hang them up to scent rooms and keep their wardrobes smelling fresh and free of moths.

The modern pomander

Pomanders are not difficult to make but the process is time-consuming. In fact, it has been rightly declared that one of the first ingredients to acquire is patience. The others are a firm Seville or bitter orange, 28g, 1oz of whole cloves with their buds intact and four tablespoons of orris root powder.

Wind a piece of tape around the orange so that it divides it into four quarters. Pin the tape into position at the top and bottom. Wearing a thimble, push the cloves closely and firmly into the orange skin, following the lines of the tape. Cover the orange with cloves until there is no skin to be seen.

Using a bowl, sift the orris root powder over the orange so that it looks like a snowball. Wrap the orange in tissue paper or muslin and place it in a paper bag (preferably brown) and keep it somewhere warm and dry for three to five weeks.

During this time, the orange will dry completely, becoming smaller and very hard. Shake off the surplus powder, and replace the tape with fresh coloured ribbon and if desired, fasten the top with a bow.

Orange pomanders are the most popular, but you can use lemons, grapefruits and limes. Orris root powder may be mixed with ground cinnamon to achieve a spicier perfume. Other recipes suggest the use of oil of bergamot and lemon verbena, which are mixed with the powder.

Fragrant Beads

An unusual way to keep the abundant fragrance of your garden roses about you all year round is to make scented beads. You can use them in many ways, as a scented necklace, wrist band, multi-stranded belt or hair decoration.

For this purpose, you will need a supply of fresh rose petals. Those from the old fashioned heavily scented varieties such as Cabbage and Damask are best, but if they are not available use petals from any dark red bloom. You will also need some essence of roses or some rose water, which can be made by infusing highly scented petals and allowing the liquid to cool overnight.

Use a pestle and mortar to crush the petals as finely as possible then spread them out on waxed paper for an hour or so to dry. Crush once again in the mortar but this time add small quantities of water to bind into a tacky paste.

Now, dip your fingers into the rose oil and using a board, roll small quantities of the paste into whatever shape and size of bead you want. After you have made a few, but before they dry, make thread holes with a strong needle.

The beads should be laid on waxed paper and turned three times a day for three days. They will then be dry and can be polished with a soft cloth.

To restore the original sweet fragrance after your beads have been in constant use, dip them in rose oil and allow to dry.

The Tussie Mussie

When the Queen makes her annual distribution of Maundy money, she, and other members of the Royal Family, carry bouquets of scented herbs and flowers called tussie mussies.

The tradition stems from the days when it was thought that the perfume of certain plants would act as a barrier against noxious smells from open drains and unwashed bodies which brought with them the risk of plague and fever. These nosegays were composed mainly of germ-repelling herbs such as rue and wormwood but later, in slightly less traumatic times, tussie mussies were used to convey messages, usually romantic.

To rue, the herb of repentance, lovers added rosemary and forget-me-nots as signs of faithfulness and lasting remembrance. Blue violets were a symbol of loyalty while white violets stood for virginity or innocence.

Publishers began producing Languages of Plants so that readers with messages of love, sympathy, disapproval or hope could convey them by carrying or sending individually designed tussie mussies on appropriate occasions.

In the Elizabethan period, tussie mussies were so popular that Shakespeare used one as a dramatic device to accentuate Ophelia's desolation in Hamlet. Following the killing of her father, she is shown making her tussie mussie and crying:

> *There's rosemary, that's for*
> *remembrance;*
> *pray you, love, remember.*
> *And there is*

> *pansies, that's for thoughts . . .*
> *There's fennel for you, and*
> *columbines.*
> *There's rue for you; and here's*
> *some for me.*
> *We may call it herb of grace a*
> *Sundays.*
> *O, you must wear rue with a*
> *difference.*
> *There's a daisy.*
> *I would*
> *give you some violets, but they*
> *wither'd all*
> *when my father died . . .*

Tracing the language of flowers in tussie mussies is a fascinating pursuit. Ophelia gave some excellent clues and no doubt the playgoers of that time would have known that fennel was for flattery and that columbines and daisies represented faithlessness.

The Language of Herbs and Flowers

If a white rose was placed on a table at an important meeting it meant that the things to be discussed were highly confidential, stemming from the rose which was

originally part of the ceiling decoration in a private chamber. This led to the expression sub-rosa.

Herbs with symbolic meanings include:

Bay—Honour (known as the herb of heroes)

Chamomile—Meekness

Fennel—Flattery

Forget-me-not—Faithfulness

Lavender—Silence

Lily of the valley—Purity

Marigold—Happiness and a sunny nature.

Marjoram—Joy

Mint—Wisdom

Pansy—Love

Parsley—Celebration

Red rose—Love

Rosemary—Remembrance

Rue—Repentance

Sage—Virtue

Thyme—Activity

White rose—Sealed lips

Making your own tussie mussie

Tussie mussies can be used for the same purpose now, as they have been for centuries. Make them for weddings, welcome home gifts, birthdays, christenings and all sorts of happy and even sad occasions. They need not be complicated, as the herbalist John Parkinson, writing in 1629 reveals. He describes a tussie mussie with a yellow flower (*Larkes Heeles*), saying that this:

> *hath a fine small scent, very pleasing, which being placed in the middle of some Carnations or Gillyflowers ... make a delicate Tussimussie, as they call it, or Nosegay, both for sight and sent.*

To make a tussie mussie, assemble the plants of your choice and strip off the lower leaves. Depending on the message you wish to convey, use a rose, a bright marigold or several heads of lavender as the centre and arrange other herbs around this. Tie the bunch neatly, but firmly, with a ribbon or strands of wool and surround this with a ring of herbs or flowers, tie again and continue in the same way with each layer.

Keep the arrangement quite

small and when it is nearly complete enclose it in an outer circle of fragrant leaves to hold it in shape. Trim the stems, stand your creation in water for a while and then finish it off with a paper doily and coloured ribbons.

If the scent of the tussie mussie is important, you will not be accused of cheating if you steep a ribbon (grosgrain) in cologne, allow it to dry, and then tie this around the arrangement. Another method is to anoint each section with a drop or two of essential oil of your choice.

A tussie mussie made like this from freshly picked herbs and flowers will keep fresh for several weeks, particularly if given a drink now and then. But after it has served its purpose, it may be hung upside down to dry and serve as a long-lasting reminder of your patience and care.

Brew Your Own Tea

Brewing a nice hot cup of tea using herbs from the garden rather than from a packet is by no means an odd or cranky activity, and has endured since man first boiled water. Modern packaged teas and coffees are comparative newcomers, but teas made from garden herbs, the French call it tisane and others call it an infusion, have been popular for centuries and have always been regarded as an aid to better health.

Even if you only have a few herbs on the windowsill, you can treat yourself to the pleasure and comfort of a gently aromatic cup of herb tea. No men in white coats will come and take you away and within weeks you will wonder why on earth you didn't start brewing your own many years earlier.

Take an ordinary teapot (not metal) and scald it before use. Strip a few leaves from your plant, break and crush them between your fingers and drop them into the pot. Cover them with boiling water, stand the pot in a warm place for about five minutes and then pour.

If you want clear liquid, use a strainer. Alternatively, you can pull a leaf or two to pieces and put these into a cup and cover with boiling water. You will probably want to spoon out the herbs before drinking.

Take things gradually, make

a simple tea from the leaves of a common herb such as mint and drink it first thing in the morning without milk. As your taste buds start adapting to the experience, jolly them along a little by adding half a teaspoon of clear honey to the cup. Then try a squeeze of lemon with the honey. Or, if the weather is hot, chill your infusion and drink it in the garden out of a frosted glass with a borage flower or two floating on the surface. Experiment further by adding a little crushed cinnamon, clove or nutmeg. Soon you will find the idea, and the taste, so attractive that you will want to broaden your tea-making horizons.

Try growing a selection of plants which were traditionally used to bring about a variety of experiences from sweet sleep to heightened alertness. If you have the space, grow enough of them to harvest and dry for use throughout the winter or to package as presents for relatives and friends.

When your birthday approaches, ask for a glass teapot so that you can see the herbs 'working' in the hot water. Or even prettier,

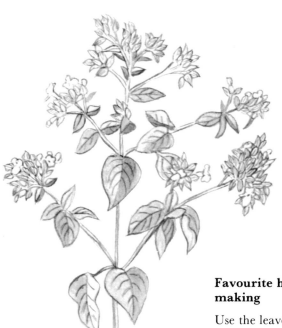

encourage someone to treat you to a lovely china teapot.

After a while you may discover that you greatly benefit from a mix of herbs or that one herb in particular is good for you. For example, if you drink sage tea you may well find you feel your age a bit less. Peppermint or lovage (seasoned with salt) might help you think more clearly. Chamomile is well known as an inducer of sleep, rosemary is said to aid the memory, and marjoram has a reputation for bringing about happiness.

Favourite herbs for tea making

Use the leaves:

Angelica—(use the young leaves) provides relief from nervous headaches.

Basil—comforts colds and eases gastric troubles.

Bergamot—a lovely drink to start the day well and yet relaxing and sleep inducing at bed-time.

Borage—a refreshing pick-me-up, very popular when served iced.

Catnip—an acquired taste but it relieves headaches.

Dandelion—this is a most important herb, according to the ancients it eased rheumatics and calmed stomach upsets.

Horehound—is excellent for wintry coughs and colds and even better with a spoonful of acacia honey.

Hyssop—not everyone's choice, but it does cleanse the system.

Lemon balm—this very popular herb tea can clear early morning sluggishness and is refreshing at any time.

Lemon verbena—a favourite, not only because of the quality of the tea it makes but because the leaves give out such a heavenly aroma that

you feel good whether you drink the concoction or not. Use just one of the smallish leaves on its own or add a leaf or two of mint.

Lovage—of broth-like consistency but particularly good for flushing the system.

Mint—it is said that mint was drunk by Eastern potentates with large harems. Still a popular and refreshing drink with aphrodisiac associations, it is surprisingly good when chilled. There are various types of mint but all have their attractions. Peppermint is good for the digestion and for relief of fatigue but is rather too pungent for many

53

tea drinkers.

Nettle—quaffed by the ancients who infused nettle tea to help purify the blood for, as the old rhyme goes:

If they would drink nettles in March
and eat Mugwort in May
So many young maidens
Wouldn't go to the clay.

Parsley—the tea is another blood purifer.

Rosemary—quietly aromatic, it helps to relieve headaches and the effects of stress.

Sage—old herbalists claimed that sage had properties which help to prolong life and kept hair from falling out. But as a pleasant drink, its praises are unsung.

Sweet Cicely—attractive to slimmers as it provides calorie-free sweetness and aids the digestive processes.

Thyme—the leaves are so small that it is best to infuse a twig or two and employ a strainer. Thyme is said to be useful for ticklish throats and sinus problems.

Vervain—highly thought of as a settler of the stomach and a natural tranquiliser, but a rather bitter drink.

Violet—makes a comforting, warming tea.

Woodruff—the tea is pleasant though not inspiring but picking the leaves is an aromatic tonic in itself.

Yarrow—like vervain, this is a slightly bitter drink, but recommended for colds and chest complaints.

Use the flowers:

Chamomile—the daisy-like flowers make a gentle aromatic aid to beauty-sleep which also helps digestion.

Coltsfoot—brew the flowers to help relieve catarrh and heaviness of the chest.

Elder—the soothing tea has a reputation for easing colds and minor throat infections.

Lime—the tea makes a refreshing nightcap.

This is just a short-list of the well tried favourites, most of them having medicinal overtones of course.

Do not feel tied to it, but experiment with a mixture of rosehips and hibiscus flowers, thirst quenching wood sorrel leaves and fennel and lovage seeds.

If you do decide to use seeds, pound them in a pestle and mortar and then simmer in boiling water for up to 10 minutes. Herb tea makers also recommend the roots of herbs such as fennel.

Aromatic
Notions

Lavender bundles

Not long ago, when a bride
assembled her trousseau, she
marked the dozens and half
dozens of items with small
bunches of lavender called
bundles or, because of the
shape, 'bottles'.

If you have a lavender
bush, and the weather is dry,
pick some long stems while
they are still fresh and pliable.
Make a neat bundle of twelve
or eighteen stalks of the
lavender, arranging the heads
altogether, and bind it just
below the heads. Taking great
care, one by one bend the
stalks back over the heads to
form a cage and after
trimming, tie them with a
coloured ribbon.

This may be improved upon
by threading a narrow ribbon
through the stalks so that the
flower heads are completely
enclosed, as in the drawing.
The weaving should be tight
at the top and bottom of the
heads but not enough to
damage the stalks.

A lavender doll

Because they are easy to make

and very acceptable as
presents, lavender dollies can
be a useful introduction for a
child to the art of cutting and
sewing.

Cut two identical
doll-shapes of flowery material
(right sides together) and sew
around the edge leaving the
bottom open. Turn the shape
inside out, stuff it with dried

lavender flowers and sew up
the bottom using tiny stitches
to ensure that the flowers do
not drop out. Attach a loop of
ribbon so that the doll may be
hung up in a cupboard to
keep moths away. Hair, face,
collar, buttons and other
features can be added
according to skill and time
available.

Aromatic tea cosy

As warmth brings out the natural perfume of herbs, you may imagine how sweet smelling a herbal tea cosy can become once covering a hot pot of tea.

Make the cosy from cotton material and wadding in any shape that pleases. When it is nearly completed make two small pockets on the inside. Into these insert two sachets of lavender flowers or powdered pot pourri.

Scented drawer liners

If you hate throwing away beautiful wrapping paper, or even pretty wallpaper use the paper as scented drawer liners.

First remove any damaged edges or sealing tape from the paper, then find a large dress box or empty drawer and place a piece of the paper flat in the box, spreading powdered pot pourri over it. Now lay your remaining sheets of paper over this and cover the whole with a lid or newspaper to contain the aroma. Shake the container gently or turn the paper once a week and within a month or so the aroma of the pot pourri will have permeated the paper.

Another way of scenting paper is to place the sheets in

59

a polythene bag and sprinkle over the powdered pot pourri. Seal the bag, give it an occasional shake and leave it unopened until you are ready to use the contents.

Scented inks and paper

Scented inks and paper might sound like the epitome of luxury, but provided you have a few aromatic herbs to hand they will cost you no more than ordinary writing materials.

For the ink, you need a herb with what one old herbalist called 'a robust scent', so rosemary is a good choice to begin with. Pluck a few stems, cut off just the tips of the small leaves and crush them with a rolling pin. Drop them into water in a small enamel saucepan and bring rapidly to the boil.

Leave the saucepan uncovered and gently simmer until most of the water evaporates and the liquid assumes a muddy brownish hue. Strain the liquid into a small jug, let it cool then add up to four teaspoons to a normal bottle of ink.

When you use the ink, you will probably notice no perfume, but the recipients of your letters will catch a subtle hint of fragrance when they open the envelope.

To scent notepaper, simply put it into a small lidded box with a sachet of pot pourri. (Include the envelopes if you wish.) Ensure the sachet is sealed or tiny specks of pot pourri dust may mar the writing surface.

Scented greeting cards

Scented greeting cards are popular with children and easy to make.

Fold a piece of card in half to form a square and cut out the front of the card to make a window. Now cut out two slightly larger circles from a coloured fabric, tack them together and insert some particularly fragrant pot pourri. Sew the two pieces together to form a sachet, and glue this to the inside of the window.

Herbal garter

Herbal garters have been worn over the centuries and even now country brides continue this charming tradition.

Take a piece of wide elastic, long enough to fit comfortably around the leg and sew the ends together to make a circle. Enclose this with two layers of pretty, loose-woven material and add a frill. Make two vertical cuts in the outer layer and into these insert small muslin sachets containing dried lavender or pot pourri.

Fruits and pincushions

Fruit-shaped pincushions which release a little fragrance whenever you pull out a pin were very popular in Victorian times but are hard to find today. They are not difficult to make. For a herby tomato, for example, you will need four squares of red felt and one of green, tracing paper, card, red and green thread and some pot pourri.

You can make all types of fruit and mix the appropriately scented pot pourri. Alternatively, sew pin cushions in the shape of cottages, ships, footballs and even dolls. Be generous with your pot pourri, the stronger smelling this is, the better.

An aromatic bookmark

The leaves of alecost or costmary have been used since the seventeenth century as book marks, especially in family bibles. They were favoured, not only for their faintly minty scent, but also because they formed a parchment-like layer in the

bible upon which family births and deaths were recorded.

The leaf retains its aroma for years and can be given a longer life with a little encouragement. Select a leaf which is well shaped and undamaged and use a flower press or place between two sheets of newspaper and press with the weight of heavy books.

Hold the leaf against a piece of golden-coloured linen

or woven fabric and cut around it leaving a margin of about ½cm, 1in. Use a hem stitch to neaten the edge. Glue the leaf to the fabric (hemside down) and place a small sheet of film over the leaf and fabric, taking care to smooth it down evenly to remove any air or creases and trim to the shape of the material. The natural fragrance of the leaf will emerge gently but noticeably through the fabric for many years.

Herbs For Your Pets

Dogs and cats have highly inquisitive noses; they can be seen wandering through a herb garden as though they owned it, heads and tails held high and obviously enjoying the heady smells.

Cats in particular appreciate herbs and their favourite is appropriately called catmint. In 1636, the herbalist Gerard wrote about catmint saying that it was so named,

> '*because cats are very much delighted herewith; for the smell of it is so pleasant unto them, that they rub themselves upon it, and wallow or tumble in it, and also feed on the branches and leaves very greedily.*'

Catmint Mouse

It is traditional for children to sew dried catmint into small balls of cloth and hang these from a chair to amuse kittens, but the idea of a catmint mouse seems to be comparatively new. A mouse complete with eyes and whiskers is possibly more fun to make and to give.

Ideally, use the leaves and flowers of the variety, *Napeta cataria*. This dries in about

three to four days when hung in large bunches in a warm place such as the kitchen or airing cupboard.

Use coloured felt or a fairly firm material for the body of the mouse (or whatever shape you decide upon) and leave a gap to insert the dried herb material. A little kapok will help you to achieve a good shape.

Give the mouse a tail to pull it by, and whiskers, cut from twine. There is no guarantee that the cat, being a cat, will co-operate, but many happy hours can be spent watching the hilarious antics of a pet with a catmint shape.

The cat's cushion

Provided it is not too sweet-smelling, cats will also take kindly to a herb-scented cushion. The mixture most likely to appeal is catmint mixed with a lemon scented thyme, lemon balm or lemon verbena. Make a powder of the dried herbs and enclose this in loose woven cloth to form a small pillow, which you then insert beneath the cover of the cushion.

Dogs are not averse to scented cushions and playthings, though catmint has no appeal to them. Any old cloth object stuffed with left-over pot pourri will hold their attention.

If you suspect that your cat or dog may be harbouring fleas, add wormwood to the herbal mix. The herb is heartily disliked by the insect population but will not detract from the pet's enjoyment of the cushion.

Herbal garlands

Wreaths are now associated with funerals, but long before Christ they were used to crown the victorious. Great poets and festive dancers wore ivy or laurel as a symbol of joy and success.

Culinary wreaths were made to decorate kitchens, particularly during the festive season, but they also marked other celebrations. Before starting, consider the purpose for your wreath. If to congratulate academic success, include laurel and ivy leaves, if celebrating Christmas use holly berries and leaves.

You can gather most of the material from your own or other people's gardens and you should be looking for such scented herbs as lavender, southernwood, wormwood, costmary (also called alecost), also scented geraniums, rosemary, sage, santolina and ambrosia. Dried whole herbs may be used but the fresh and highly aromatic effect will be less dramatic.

You will need a wire circular shape of about 22cms, 9in in diameter and moss, (both readily available at flower shops). You can save time and trouble by buying a ring of foam material but this will not last from year to year.

67

Fill the wire with damp (not dripping) moss and secure this by binding it tightly with green string in a criss-cross pattern. Complete the garland by pushing sprigs of herbs into the damp moss until you achieve a satisfactory result. The criss-crossing of the string may provide some ideas for patterns. Keep the centre free so that there is a definite circle and try to achieve a neat, rather than bushy appearance.

Warding Off Insects

It is fortunate that a handful of herbs which smell sweet to us are very unappealing to moths and other household pests. This has long been realized, of course. The herbalist Nicholas Culpeper argued that wormwood:

> being laid among cloaths will make moth scorn to meddle with the cloaths as much as a lion scorns to meddle with a mouse, or an eagle with a fly.

By using wormwood and a choice of many other highly aromatic herbs in cupboards and drawers these tiny menaces can be excluded at the same time as keeping, clothes, curtains, carpets, bed-linen, table cloths, towels and other items fresh and fragrant the whole year round.

Herbs with a reputation for discouraging insects are: basil, bay, costmary, elder, germander, hyssop, lavender, meadowsweet, mint, pennyroyal, rosemary, rue, santolina, savory, southernwood, tansy, woodruff, and wormwood.

The herbs will work well if hung in small bunches in wardrobes or laid under newspaper in drawers and cupboards. If they are allowed a current of air they will dry well and quickly and will continue to do their job for many months. If they are then taken down, crushed and packed into small cloth bags (18cm × 13cm, 5in × 3in), they will act as insect repellents for many more years.

Lavender is best kept separately but a mix of some of the other herbs with half a teaspoon per bag of powdered cloves or violet scented orris root is highly effective. Experiment with other combinations of herbs and spices and you will soon find one that pleases you most.

One old French recipe calls for a cup each of dried rosemary, tansy. thyme, mint, southernwood, and half a cup of ground cloves. Place the mixture into small muslin bags and tie with coloured ribbon.

It is said that bay leaves laid under paper about two to a drawer will discourage troublesome insect invaders including silverfish and cockroaches.

While most people are attracted to the natural perfumes of herbs, men frequently draw the line at going to school or work with clothing smelling of lavender. The problem can be solved by keeping lavender out of their closets, but if they object to the smell of herbs altogether try sewing some small cloth bags and filling these with shavings of cedar wood and powdered sassafras root.

Anti-moth bars are another solution. Make these by taking 28g, 1oz of melted paraffin wax and stirring into this one tablespoon of heliotrope oil, a quarter teaspoon of bergamot oil and a few drops of clove oil. Blend the mixture, pour it into a flat wooden or enamel dish, allow to cool and then slice it into bars for use in closet or drawer.

Attractively packaged, these make unusual and useful little gifts.

Another masculine aroma which unsettles the moths is a combination of equal amounts of lemon peel, crushed cloves, spearmint and tansy, sewn into bags and placed among clothes. More simply, just place the dried rhizomes of the herb sweet flag or elecampane among your precious woollens and other clothes.

The old practice of laying (strewing) sweet flag and scented herbs like pennyroyal over floors to ward off fleas is out-dated, but there is much to be said for temporary strewing in areas infested with ants and silverfish.

Catnip is also effective when dried and sprinkled around the ant trails while sprigs of southernwood and costmary, placed under a carpet, will keep moths away.

Bay in the larder

Bay leaves in and among the storage jars will evict pests and discourage weevils. Other herbs of particular use are tansy, hung in the cupboard doorway to keep bluebottles at bay, and pennyroyal and rue on the shelves to ward off ants and other trespassers.

One proven method of keeping insects out of the house is to hang freshly cut herbs with insect repellent qualities at all entrances. Many people regard it as quite natural to hang large bunches at doorways, open windows and even in the fireplaces in summer.

In the winter, when your guard can be dropped and the herbs have dried, break up the bunches and spread over the blazing fire to bring some of the aromas of summer back to the home.

An old Herefordshire remedy is to fill small mesh bags with a mixture of clover flowers, well broken bay leaves, crushed cloves and eucalyptus leaves and hang these at all entrances.

As well as hanging herbs at entrances to the house, it is also useful to plant them around doorways. Pennyroyal is a good plant for this purpose as it thrives between paving stones and when trodden upon releases a wonderful scent and continues to flourish.

Basil, grown in a pot on the window-sill, will give most flies their marching orders and if accompanied by marigolds in another pot will warn off many greenhouse pests as well.

Fragrant Surprises

There is a story that in the seventeenth century an Eastern princess asked that the canal route taken by the barge after her wedding should be scattered with rose petals. Her father had roses gathered from miles around and the water was filled with the petals of Damask and other roses. After the ceremony, as the wedding party departed, the royal couple allowed their hands to trail in the water. So delighted were they by the sweetly scented oil left on their hands, that they charged the royal perfumer to reproduce

the fragrance. Thus the famous attar (or otto) of roses was created.

Today, oils are commercially distilled from hundreds of plants. While you cannot set up your own distillery you can extract herbal or floral oil without complicated equipment.

A worthwhile attar of roses, takes almost two hundred pounds of roses for an ounce

of oil, and requires strong sunlight for weeks on end, so it would be more practicable to make a floral oil.

Rise early on a sunny morning and collect the very best of the petals of such sweet scented flowers as sweet peas, violets, geraniums and honeysuckle. Place in a clean ceramic pot and just cover them with clean rain water or a bottle of still spring water (never use tap water). Stand the pot in the full sun and eventually the water will develop a film, which is your precious oil.

Collect the oil by dabbing it with cotton wool and squeezing it into a clean glass container. When you have done so, cover this container with a couple of layers of cheesecloth which excludes dirt but allows any water in the container to evaporate. After a few days, pour the oil into a sterilized glass jar or bottle with a close-fitting lid and store this away from the light until you need it.

Herbal oils are made by the same method from the unblemished leaves and seeds of such aromatic herbs as angelica, basil, dill, marjoram, mint, rosemary, sage, thyme and woodruff.

Perfume essences

If you wear perfume, make a natural perfume essence to fit your mood. Saturate cotton wool with highly refined olive oil (sweet oil), and place in a glass jar, adding sweet smelling flowers and leaves. Close the lid tightly and leave the jar in the sun or in a warm place for a day and a night. Turn out the plant material, add freshly picked flowers and

leaves. Carry on doing this day after day for a week or so, keeping the lid tight shut. When you think the oil has absorbed sufficient scent, squeeze the cotton wool to release the fragrance-laden oil into a glass container. Keep it in a refrigerator.

Taking the waters

Although herb-based cosmetics are attracting interest, cosmetic waters which you can make in your home for next to nothing can keep you looking fit and well. An occasional splash will stimulate the skin and keep it toned, clean, fresh and sweet smelling. All you need is spring, rain or distilled water and whatever fragrant flowers and leaves are available.

Rose water

Much-loved rose water is made by placing freshly gathered rose petals in an enamel pan, just covering them with water and slowly bringing the mixture to the boil. Simmer for about ten minutes, then strain it into a jug or bottle.

Chamomile water, which helps to firm skin tissue and halt the advance of wrinkles, is made by soaking the flowers in water and shaking twice

73

daily for a fortnight. It should then be strained and bottled.

Use the blender to make a purée of fresh water and herb leaves. The aromatic mint is particularly effective where a refreshing 'dab' is required.

Grow Your Own Herbs

If you have a garden, it should not be difficult to find a corner in which to grow a few herbs. Unless you have plenty of space, leave the growing of space-consuming herbs like angelica to others and concentrate on less expansive plants. By limiting the number of herbs you start growing, you can give each plant sufficient attention and become better aquainted with it.

Select a patch or border which catches the sun for much of the day and is not overshadowed by a tree. Generally speaking, herbs are very tolerant but they do like any available warmth and moisture.

Ideally, your herbs should be in easy reach so you can watch their progress and pick the leaves and flowers just when they are ready.

If no garden space is available, herbs will flourish in tubs provided they are given good soil and not allowed to dry out. With a little tender loving care, they will also grow well in window boxes and may even be brought indoors for a while. Tender

herbs such as lemon verbena, pineapple sage and bay appreciate cover during the cold weather and vegetate happily near a window in a draught and frost-free room.

Herbs can be brought on successfully on a window sill but should not be expected to spend their whole lives there. During their stay they must be kept out of draughts and sprinkled with rain-water once a day. Over-watering, particularly with tap water, can be fatal.

Seeds and cuttings
Some of the herbs you will need for pot pourri can be started from seed, which you sow directly into the ground or in trays in the spring. But a

great many can be bought as plants to transfer directly into the soil. When the herb has matured, you may take cuttings to increase your stock or dig up the root and divide it into growing sections.

Generally speaking, herbs will increase themselves quite rapidly by dropping seeds or, like mint, sending out runners from which offsprings grow. Keep only those you know you will need and discard any that will not give you the aroma or colour you want.

Time for harvest
Your object in gathering herbs is to retain as much as possible of the essential oil. The ideal time is in the morning, after the dew has disappeared, but before the sun is in full spate.

Leaves are usually at their best before the flowers come into bloom and roots are ripe in the autumn. Handle them carefully to prevent bruising and loss of oil. Gather flowers when they are open but before they are full blown. Lavender needs to be harvested while the florets are still closed, or most of the scent will be lost.

Seeds and seedheads should be ripe, but not so dry that they fall to the ground when touched. Catch them just before then, and hang them up in a brown paper bag to dry. Pick only the best, for damp and diseased material will look unsightly and contaminate anything it touches.

Drying herbs

It is possible to dry herbs successfully in a micro-wave oven, but the aroma is retained less well.

One of the few rules for drying is to ensure a circulation of air. Because of this, herbs should be tied in small bunches as large ones encourage damping off in the centre. Hang these up in the warm air or place them on a drying frame made of muslin slung like a series of hammocks.

A spare shelf in a greenhouse is ideal, provided air circulates and the material is not allowed to become scorched. One of the best methods, as described earlier, is to place newspaper on a bedroom floor and allow the herbs and rose petals to dry gently over several days.

Plant material is regarded as dry when it is papery or, as one writer described it, not unlike a cornflake. Leaves should be brittle but should not shatter.

Always be sure to store dried material where it cannot absorb moisture, or it will be ruined. Tight-fitting lids are essential.

Pot Pourri Recipes

Queen of the Garden

This lends a highly invigorating aroma, most suitable for scenting a larger room. You will need:

1 cup of lemon verbena leaves
½ cup of violet flowers
½ cup of rose geranium leaves
and flowers
1 tablespoon of grated lemon
peel.

For a fixative, use either a teaspoon of clary sage leaves or the same amount of orris root powder.

   You need not stick too slavishly to the quantities given here or in the following recipes. They are set out to provide you with what is referred to as 'a rough balance' from which you can develop. There are few rules to follow in making pot pourri which means there is room for experimentation—and surprise.

Bath Vinegar

For the bath a special vinegar will make you feel as fresh as a daisy. The ingredients you will need are:

½ pint (300 ml) of cider
vinegar
½ pint (300 ml) of spring
water
3 tablespoons of fresh herbs;
rosemary, fennel, lavender,
comfrey and chamomile are
obvious candidates.

Mix the vinegar and water together and heat until nearly boiling. Add the herbs and leave them to steep overnight. Strain, then bottle. You should add about half a pint, 300 ml of the liquid to each bath.

Sweet Linen

This simpler mixture is ideal for putting into muslin bags which can be placed among sheets, pillowslips and clothing to give them a wonderful fresh scent. You will need:

1 cup of crumbled leaves of roses
1 tablespoon of ground cloves
1 tablespoon of ground seeds of caraway
1 tablespoon of ground allspice
$\frac{1}{2}$ cup of well dried salt

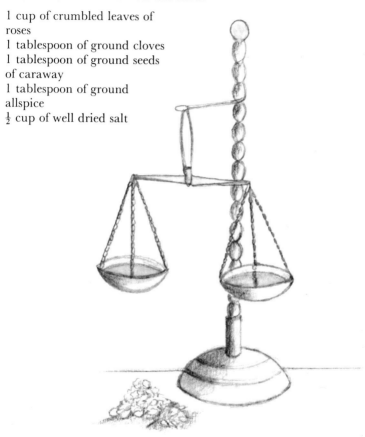

Make sure you mix the ingredients thoroughly and follow the pot pourri making instructions given earlier. When spices are called for in a recipe, try to obtain them whole and as fresh as possible. Break them up with a pestle and mortar or in a coffee mill or beat them with a small hammer in a wooden bowl.

Harem Nights

This is a truly exotic mixture but patience is required in finding all the ingredients, some of which are a little more unusual. Ask in health food or ethnic stores in the area.

$\frac{1}{2}$ cup of bruised root of sweet
flag
$\frac{1}{2}$ cup (or a little under) of
yellow sandalwood
1 tablespoon of cedarwood
1 tablespoon of cloves
1 tablespoon of nutmeg
1 tablespoon of patchouli
leaves

You will also need about half a cup of orris root powder and a tablespoon each of storax and benzion. All three are fixatives and their combination is powerful indeed. Orris root is the powdered rhizome of the Florentine iris while storax and benzion are gums collected from trees. To find all three would be a worthwhile achievement.

Golden Time

This again is a simple mix but its 'dry' scent always gives pleasure. You will need:

$\frac{1}{2}$ cup of thyme leaves
$\frac{1}{2}$ cup of peppermint leaves
$\frac{1}{2}$ cup of basil leaves
$\frac{1}{2}$ cup of marigold petals
4 drops of oil of peppermint
$\frac{1}{4}$ cup of orris root powder

When looking at pot pourri recipes in old books, which makes a peaceful pastime on a rainy day, you will find pot pourri measurements are given in many ways, including teaspoonfuls and handfuls. As mentioned earlier, the trick is to achieve the right balance so that you have sufficient of one ingredient yet not enough to overpower another.

Hair Rinse

Simple rinses to brighten hair and give it a glossy appearance can be made in minutes. Those with dark hair will need a handful of rosemary leaves; those with fair hair will require a handful of chamomile flowers.

Pour about 1¾ pints, 1 litre of boiling water over the leaves and steep for another 30 minutes. Strain into an earthenware jug through muslin. Cover and allow to cool. Use as a final rinse after shampooing by pouring it over your hair into a basin, repeating the process several times.

National Trust
Rose and Herb Gardens to Visit

Rose Gardens
Ascott
Buckinghamshire

Bateman's
East Sussex (planted by
Kipling)

Chartwell
Kent (planted by Lady
Churchill)

Cliveden
Buckinghamshire

Grey's Court
Oxfordshire

Hidcote Manor Garden
West Sussex

Mottisfont Abbey
Hampshire

Nymans Garden
West Sussex

Peckover House
Cambridgeshire

Plas Newydd
Anglesey

Polesden Lacey
Surrey

Shugborough
Staffordshire

Wallington
Northumberland

Herb Gardens

Acorn Bank
Cumbria

Bateman's
East Sussex

Bradley Manor
Devon

Buckland Abbey
Devon

Gunby Hall
Lincolnshire

Hardwick Hall
Derbyshire

Scotney Castle
Kent

Springhill
County Londonderry